Not

poems by

Grove Koger

Finishing Line Press
Georgetown, Kentucky

Not

ACKNOWLEDGMENTS

"Scape" originally appeared in *Poetica Review* and was reprinted in *Boise
Spoken Word Collective*
"The Meteor" originally appeared in *Wordland*
"Long Distance," "Odd," and "Envoi" originally appeared in *Cold-Drill*
"Not" originally appeared in *Cold-Drill* and was reprinted in *Stray Branch*
"Out Here the Distances" originally appeared in *Cold-Drill* and was
reprinted in *Synaeresis: Arts + Poetry*
"Now" originally appeared in *Poetica Review*
"The Door" originally appeared in *Rat's Ass Review*
"Playing near You" originally appeared in *The Limberlost Review* and was
reprinted in *Altered Reality Magazine*
"Enigma" originally appeared in *Cold-Drill and* was reprinted in *The
Fabulist, Twist in Time* and *Boise Spoken Word Collective*
"He Remembers" originally appeared in *Cabin Fever* and was reprinted in
Boise Spoken Word Collective
"The Weather There" originally appeared in *Cabin Fever*

Publisher: Leah Huete de Maines
Editor: Christen Kincaid
Cover Art: Byron Cavender
Author Photo: Margaret Koger
Cover Design: Elizabeth Maines McCleavy

Order online: www.finishinglinepress.com
also available on amazon.com

Author inquiries and mail orders:
Finishing Line Press
PO Box 1626
Georgetown, Kentucky 40324
USA

Contents

Dedicated to the Memory of My Parents

Scape

River knows
the way, run
away, don't
stay.

Rock knows
the way: Come
what may, stay.
Stay.

The Meteor

When my mother was young
she visited Charleston
and saw something marvelous
late one evening:
a meteor streaking up
out of the east
seemingly out of the water
out of the black Atlantic
and rising to the zenith
where it disintegrated
        silently
into a dozen smaller meteors that
disappeared in the pale west.

This would have been
shortly before she met my father
        but another time
when she retold the story
it was shortly afterward.

Then another time she saw the meteor in
Savannah.

Perhaps she dreamt the meteor
and after a time it became real.
Or perhaps I dreamt it
and gave the memory to her.
Perhaps she'll visit me tonight
in my sleep to thank me
for giving her
such a marvelous memory.

Long Distance

Months later I heard you
and your voice was so clear
that it shattered the windows and
the winter swept in
around me

Not

Not the boxes of photographs of people I never knew, stiff in their shabbiness.

Not summer on the farm I grew up on.
Not the apples and apricots and plums that weighed down the limbs of the trees of my early childhood.

Not the friends I never saw again, whose faces I lost, whose names became the words of the song I sang myself to sleep with.

Not the preternatural silence of dawn.
Not the black night sliding down like the curtain after the first act of the unfolding drama of the rest of your life.

Not the surprise of sex.
Not your fingers busy at my groin.
Not the surprise of waking up alone, or of not waking up alone.
Not love or lust.

Not the things you can't remember, and not the things you can.
Not coffee roasting before daylight.
Not the squids fried crisp and hung up in the cruel sun, not yogurt and honey on the terrace or the scorpion dreaming on the plaster wall.
Not sand so hot you couldn't walk, and not the cold sea boiling up all the way from Calabria.
Not the sting of ouzo.

Not year in and year out.
Not the arguments about none of the things that mattered.
Not the words we didn't say.
Not the sights we didn't see.
Not the tree that fell again and again in the forest.
Not the tears that never fell.
Not sentiment.
Not the dust that gathered in the corners of all the rooms of all the houses we never went back to.

Not the peristalsis of thought.
Not the *Cloud of Unknowing.*
Not the First Cause or the Last Four Things.
Not the parades.
Not the Bill of Rights or the Hammer and Sickle or "La Marseillaise."
Not the Eiffel Tower, not the Académie Française, not the Popular Front.
Not Unter den Linden.
Not the Spanish Civil War or the Lincoln Brigade.

Not cold marble.
Not the Parthenon, not the Tower of Babel, not the Ziggurat of Ur.
Not the Pyramid of Khufu or the Colossus of Rhodes or the other five wonders of the ancient fucking world.

Not the deliquescence of history or the green putrescence of culture, busy with maggots.

Not the Magellanic Clouds.
Not cosmic dust afloat beyond Aldebaran.
Not x-rays escaping the Crab Nebula at 186,282 miles per second.

Not absolute zero.

Not anticipation.
Not disappointment.

Not the words on the page.

Not the words not on the page.

Out Here the Distances

In nineteen and twelve the
nearest neighbor was
an hour's ride away. If you
was so sick you needed a doctor
fast, you was a dead man, and
decent firewood meant
three days in the hills with
a wagon and team. They
was so many trees, Uncle Bob
would tell me years later, and
as I looked up he spread
his hands from horizon to
horizon.

But I burn every
photograph I can lay my hands
on. I don't want to be
reminded of Uncle Bob and those
boys of his, or that team he kept,
or that puppy of his I beat
because I dreamed it bit
me.

Out here the
distances never change. There
are new neighbors now, and
closer, but they keep to
themselves. These days
I have firewood delivered, and
I swear to God it burns just as
brightly.

Now

It is what it is,
your doctor says,
and you nod. And
before long
it was what it was,
whatever it was.
Or maybe not.

Time passes and now
something else is
what it is, whatever that is.
Don't ask.

Stuff happens and
we shake our heads.
Huh!

There are bigger words,
I know. Better words,
more precise—but
none good enough to
paper over this crack in
the world.

Odd

    Odd
how the fender that
broke the doe's back so
easily that night
pleated like foil against
the canyon wall.

                I
don't like
thinking about these
things, you know,
but they're thinking
about me.

The Door

The door never shut tight,
was warped, maybe,
or the jamb was crooked.
Or the foundation was settling.
Who knows?

We called in our old carpenter,
but when he couldn't fix it
we said,
Never mind.

We were young and impatient.

But did that door
let in everything that
followed?

Playing near You

They've scheduled
the end of everything, and
I just thought
you'd want to know.

We're all invited, although
naturally there'll be
a limited number of
front-row seats available on
a first-come, first-served basis.
If I were you, I'd
act now. They're predicting
standing room only.

The light show is
going to be
out of this world, and
the sound, well, they tell
me the sound is unbelievable.
Forget the previews, this
is guaranteed to be
the real thing. Unique.

There'll be one showing only.
It's the end of everything,
and I know you'll want
to be there.

Enigma

Having arrived at last
you will never have left,

will you?

And those spires
dancing in the afternoon heat
are the spires of
the palace of dreams,

aren't they?

And the deserted quay,
and the empty sky,
and the boats drawn up
in the sand,

the gale forever
threatening, forever receding—

they all, all appear
on the stamp on the letter
you mailed yourself
last night in your sleep,

don't they?

Didn't they?

Won't they?

He Remembers

She brought one cat West with her,
and a coyote got it
the first week. Then
as the times changed it was
the neighbors' dogs, and finally
their damn pickups. I was there
the day she ran down to the
road to find old Jiggs in
the borrow pit.

When her world finally
shrank to a single room,
she'd sit staring at them. *All
my cats,* she'd say in a proud
voice. You could still hear
the South in it. *All
my cats.*

Her room was perfectly bare.

Now she's left me all her cats.
They slink in one by one
to fill my room at night,
a larger room
in a far grander house
in a bigger town.
They perch in the windows,
watching me sleep, and
will not go away.

The Weather There

The dead call
late at night but never
have much to say.

How're the kids?
How's the wife?
How's the dog?

The weather there
is always cloudy, it seems.
It may rain, but then again
maybe not.

The dead always call
late at night, and I
don't have much to say to them
either. The silence
is a little awkward.
Finally I tell them I'll
see them soon and
hang up.

Envoi

After a final daring performance
without a net
before an audience of thousands
the tightrope walker bowed deeply and
flew away

Idaho native **Grove Koger** is the author of *When the Going Was Good: A Guide to the 99 Best Narratives of Travel, Exploration, and Adventure*; Assistant Editor of *Deus Loci: The Lawrence Durrell Journal*; former Assistant Editor of *Art Patron Magazine*; and former Contributing Editor for *Books with Boise Magazine*. His fiction has appeared in such publications as *Cirque, La Piccioletta Barca, Punt Volat,* and *The Bosphorus Review of Books,* and his nonfiction in *The Limberlost Review, Amsterdam Quarterly,* and *The Philadelphia Review of Books.*

Koger worked as Director of the Meridian (Idaho) Free Library District and as a reference librarian at Boise Public Library and Albertsons Library, Boise State University, and in the latter capacity received the 1999 Allie Beth Martin Award from the Public Library Association and Baker & Taylor for demonstrating an "extraordinary range and depth of knowledge about books or other library materials" as well as a "distinguished ability to share that knowledge." He lives in Boise with his wife, poet Margaret Koger.

www.ingramcontent.com/pod-product-compliance
Lightning Source LLC
Chambersburg PA
CBHW022110080426
42734CB00009B/1547